SPRING SONNETS

ALSO BY DON YORTY

A Few Swimmers Appear
Poet Laundromat
What Night Forgets

SPRING SONNETS

DON YORTY

© 2019 Don Yorty
Cover and text art: Ahm Akram
Book design: adam b. bohannon
Book editor: Lisa DeSiro
Published by Indolent Books,
an imprint of Indolent Arts Foundation, Inc.
www.indolentbooks.com
Brooklyn, New York
ISBN: 978-1-945023-22-4

Special thanks to EPIC SPONSOR Megan Chinburg for helping to fund the production of this book.

for my father
who enjoyed these sonnets
and thought they had promise

I

Looking at the springs, sitting in the sun
something at my nape begins to tickle
like the wind's moving a hair there, fickle
on my bare neck between the scalp and trunk.
I'm reading the poet Bill Kushner—Ah!
His April Poems are wonderful to hold.
It's April and I'm here with Bill—But no.
Something's crawling on my skin. Is it? What?
I scratch and it vanishes like a thought
forgotten, but it's not. It walks. I pick
from my neck a beautiful round red tick
with many tiny moving legs, enough
to turn my thoughts from Bill to blood and death.
It knows I'm here, where I wanted to rest.

2

Every time I come it is the same, stream
running without end down the mountain stairs
rocks, giant eggs and heads of dinosaurs.
Elegant woods, soft, expanding gently
over everything, a promised dream
of health, happiness, not bombed little kids
without limbs, politicians getting rich
off suffering—Away! I want to be
among unfolding ferns and skunk cabbage
where the warm bright sun thaws the ground still cold
like Christ raising Lazarus. As I grow
old it seems possible to really love
even the startled snake scared in the leaves
but man—Who threw this bottle in the stream?

3

Silent morning, about to rain. Birds sing
conversations in the willows. One lone
dove coos and makes everything beautiful.
Cachito, quiet at my feet's sleeping
curled, paws over his nose, pointed dark ear.
Now I hear a bus down Avenue C
vanish, gone in its fumes. Voices appear
coming home or off to work. Way up here
I was happy, not a thing did I want
or fear unsure of what was real or not
then I heard my voice talking to myself
then the twittering of birds then a dove
then shouts of someone crazy on the block.
I thought I was alone, but I am not.

4

Jimmy, you let your dogs shit where they want
and you don't pick it up. It is your fault
when unsuspecting others come and walk
through the crap or their toddlers catch some bug.
But you're the one who's most unfortunate.
I would rather not have lived than be you.
What you do to others you do to you
and your dog's shit's the very least of it.
I think you've not been loved; you steal, don't give.
Once I wanted to kill you with a rock
smash your head in behind the hill—And fuck
no one would have known, but I let you live
and though I know your suffering's thorough
it's still my fault it's not a better world.

5

When I think of all the lovers I've had
it's a blur, I'm afraid, of quantity
but there was quality in quantity
angels found in the common crowd, riffraff
whose amorous wings, far from this fact called earth
took me up in heavenly abstraction
from the orgy really to the action
of orgasm when remembered or birth
or flame or premonition, Adam Eve.
Who can tell us what has been? For love you
have to wait, be as chosen as a Jew.
Love's not Godot though and fortunately
when I think of Love's smile softly I can
remember those lips. Whose? I've forgotten.

6

The flies and itching heat are gone at last.
Lovely autumn, just a walk from my door
golden and energetic, I adore
you here with me steadfast as the promise
of middle age. Birds rustle in the leaves.
Or are they footsteps coming from behind?
No, it's only a squirrel I turn to find
close to the bench as unafraid of me
by the East River in East River Park
which was built from the rubble of London
bombed, brought back, ballast in the emptied hulls
of battleships returning to New York
in World War II. Who really knows what was?
Brown and yellow, red they fall, spring's green buds.

7

You weren't the sort of friend to come and go.
Then one day the spit dribbled down your chin
and your chapped lips that never stopped talking
of Raphael and Michelangelo
grew silent. I knew that you had suffered
more than I could know though I know one day
perhaps I'll know. Right now I don't. I'd say
"Do you want us to say The Lord's Prayer
together?" It seemed to give you comfort.
Oh the nonsense of this world! Who can't see
that we all come to this, both enemy
and friend? It is so absurd not to love
love till the end. In my pen when the ink
runs out, are my thoughts somehow diminished?

8

We met by chance in a shadowy place
not too far from the sea with enough light
that we could look each other in the eye
while another bent over your phallus
whom you left then abandoned in the dark
like peeling off a layer of your lust
to come to me, the kernel of yourself
directly, not stopping. I was the mark
the spot, all calm, the center of your storm
invulnerable place found in a dream
where you could unclothe and embrace. You seemed
like a friend I was seeing again or
a familiar stranger who somehow knows
the silent tender acquaintance of souls.

9

When I put headphones on it's like I'm deaf.
The world goes by silently on its own
like schools of fish in an aquarium
or New Yorkers who appear to my left
my right a little bit like trash or leaves
scattered by a thoughtless wind. I am not
alone but it feels that way without sound
until my CD spins Carlos Vives
singing, clapped to my head, his song the world
all that there is: Colombian rhythms
that move my hips and rump along with them
till in my ears and all around me whirls
even the stranger who sits down to rest
drawn from the soundless crowd to this park bench.

10

To know the truth we need to talk and read.
Two at least must do it, talker talker
writer reader revealing things that we
already know so absolutely sure
of our own selves because somebody else
was there to tell us. Ramón Jiménez
I know I lived because you did. You help
me see all that I am, the new sunset
sunrise, butterfly and happy sparrow
whose God's the blue sky, the unparalleled
burro whose life's like mine, joy and sorrow
light and shadow reflected in the well.
You can talk to friends even when they're dead.
Their voices appear like words from a pen.

II

Work will overcome evil like the grass
covers dirty hypodermic needles
dog shit and broken glass. Good does prevail
while evil's jagged edge is dulled at last.
Anarchists threw bottles to hear them crash
and never bothered, spoiled brats, to sweep it up
not blaming themselves when children don't come
but let their pit bulls tear the tire to trash
where children used to swing. All day long they
gerrymandered the park bench to drink, drug
take a long piss when the beer filled them up.
Parasites can't pervade a healthy place.
Work scared away the lazy, forgotten
and children play where they once vomited.

14

I'm happy when the day begins and I'm
happy when it ends. I like to wake up
and start again and I like to sleep. Does
this mean I'll be happy dead or alive?
The morning sun shines warmly on my head
through the cold window. I'm reading a book.
People get kidnapped, kidnappers wear hoods.
It's tense and sad by García Márquez.
Interspersed with a few ironic laughs
shadows of ladybugs move on the page
elongate words, cast from the windowpane
where they really crawl. An old lady has
to be taken out and shot. I could cry
as the year's trespassed by the new and flies.

15

It is snowing, it snowed, and it will snow
but the city won't cancel public school.
I have to go to work, something I do
whether I'm paid to or not. It is cold
outside. "Inside is warm." Did I say that
before or was it something that I dreamed?
Warm's a good sound. I teach people to speak
English. We know from opposites like cat
and dog, happy, sad, right, wrong, night and day.
Don't be afraid; we learn from our mistakes.
Repeat after me, "We all strive to say
the same thing." We understand and translate.
We laugh and say, "In the land of the blind
the man who is king has only one eye."

16

The setting sun and I are way above
the clouds and far below us I can see
the snowy ground. A man in front of me
puts headphones on. Almost everyone
is watching the movie. I see the earth's
a dark coal, a dying ember. The west
glows red and thin till it like the thinnest
eyelid closes and the day's gone, a dearth.
My destination is Salt Lake where friends
and perhaps fame await. In the window
I see myself transparent as a ghost
staring through my reflection. The heaven
grows dark with light. From a crevice of clouds
a star comes out and shines in my eye now.

19

My hands are numb and yet the sun is bright.
It's early spring when death becomes alive.
Crows caw, geese honk, and the mallards quack at
the pond. The ice is gone, but at the back
of the barn there still was snow to be found
looking just like white flowers on the ground.
March and April are my favorite time.
Cold youth thinking only of itself smiles
as attractive as the photos of my
parents, young sailor and his happy bride
who has grown old and struggles up the steps
I slowly rise behind waiting to step
into the kitchen which is warm unlike
the waking yard outside stabbed with wild chives.

20

Just as I write two hawks above the trees
fly fast away. Shadow of a buzzard
passes over my shoulder hopefully.
I was expecting rain, impeded start
but the sun's come out, made the day open
as a pursued lover turning might smile
and kiss me on the mouth. Surprised I am
chosen I am happy as can be while
everything gets worse. Soldiers still fight
in Afghanistan and Iraq, two wars
I hadn't wanted, but then who am I?
The wind blows my pages while I write for
those killed in battle. Wind, give me the breath
the word eternal not alive or dead.

21

The butterflies of spring are small and dark
not colorful and bright like butterflies
of summer hovering from flower to flower
in beauty's camouflage. Two butterflies
on the asphalt road laid with silver stone
though small stand out. Because they're dark I see
wings lined with white flutter and rise up, gone
in blurry jagged flight through the bare trees
whose branches, rusty buds blow in the wind.
There I lose sight of them like a prayer
vanishes when other thoughts intrude. In
the woods a bird whistles and I'm aware
of the three notes, a path I do not know
although I've walked here many times before.

22

The fortunate fish escaped from the net
knows what it's like to go to heaven.
Is life the net? Is that what Buddha meant?
Are the holes in the hands the nails nail in
not only bleeding, but open, the wound
the way out? No one answers the question
what is it like to be dead? Very soon
those we love are and we do follow them
going where love goes though it be the end.
In Iraq they say militants kidnapped
three Japanese humanitarians
and plan to set them on fire. More yet
yes much more suffering. Will it ever
stop? The wise may stop, the world never.

24

The sun is bright reflected on water
shimmering it to pieces. With too much
light I'm blind. They say when we see God
up close we die. I'm pretty sure I've never
looked on God up close but every day
along the way see God in every face.
We try to add God up in countless space
and God keeps coming. Generations, waves
burn around the Statue of Liberty
ripple and sparkle the Hudson River
lapping its fire right up to me. We are
all in flames and existence I can see
flies up completely still on outspread wings
a seagull hovering against the winds.

25

My cat and I play chasing each other.
He jumps while I write and then stretches out
full length in back of the warm computer
to claw my hand when it comes in sight. Ouch!
Ow! I say but Cachito doesn't care
about a little cry. Now if I die
and go to heaven, it wouldn't be fair
if Cachito dead and gone couldn't fly
to meet me. Hand in paw forever
like friends jumping from the World Trade Center
or tourists who're caught in stormy weather
we will go or we won't go together
having fun. What's a little blood? I scratch.
Cachito bites me and I bite him back.

28

Writing's a thing of opposites, putting
on clothes, taking them off, whispering shouts
starting a fire and then putting it out.
You don't want to burn the pages. Writing
flames, when words are on fire, they take flight
toward the horizon in an open mind
and they're more combustible when they rhyme.
Very much like birds words fly out of sight
before us on our journey. What's thinking
but flying, following thoughts? Why are they
always words? Love's the word I strive to say
to you, believing it the place where striving
ceases, there pain ends, and even the best
of words. Love we'll remember after death.

30

In the early dewdrop chilly morning
I'm alone gardening. What a delight!
It's been hot and noisy. Now's a quiet
tranquil dawn. New York City's still sleeping
tired out. It was loud. Don't wake the city.
I want to hear waking in La Plaza
beds of dark roses and gladiolas
sparrows chirping in the willows. Beauty's
a lot of work and Manhattan's landscape's
a flower itself of stone, desire and sweat.
Yes I am determined and alive yet
with time to spare, but not one hour to waste.
Reader, you might not know this ages hence
but my hands are dirty as I write this.

31

Today for the first time in my whole life
I can't find the phone. Where did I put it?
I'm so confused that it scares me. I quit.
Am I crazy? This is way too much strife.
Maybe it's Alzheimer's. Attached to cords
you could follow you'd find phones at their ends
in the old days. Now they're where you put them.
When I see people talk to themselves or
gesticulate in the street they are not
necessarily nuts but on their phones
talking to someone else. No one's alone
anymore. Times change. There's nothing about
it you can do, but if you don't change, you
don't move, and you're run down by the future.

32

A cawing crow gets louder and louder
invisible bird disturbing my thoughts.
Another joins in and one becomes us
as I too am drawn in and get closer
taken up in a fight in a tree top
about what? Shut up! Life's a clamor, more
unexpected than not, discordant more
than concordant that won't stop till it stops.
The cawing crows turn into splashing cars
on the nearby highway. It rained all night
lightning and thundered, noises that I like
when I'm warm, inside, and the storm is far.
Ah! there's a lull quiet as my cat is
watching for moles and mice by the trellis.

36

I see how strong a fragile thing can be.
Look! A butterfly comes fluttering
over its own reflection hovering
out in the middle of a pond so deep
and close you'd think no insect strength could last
the distance needed to reach land, yet up
it goes above the wide-mouthed bass that jumps
and death itself waits for it to stick fast
get soggy and drown. A visible song
singing against all odds in gusts of wind
that ought to knock it down, it's carried in
every limb beyond the half-sunk log
coming to spread its beating wings and soar
vanishing in the branches on the shore.

37

I overturned the rowboat planning soon
to row, looking as I turned it over
for water snakes or wasps in their paper
nests, but there was nothing there, it was true
so I reached out to get the oars and saw
appearing in a quiet growing swarm
hornets in their orbits out of the warm
earth from a hole all in alarm and awe.
Around where I had plunked the old boat down
waking them up to come out and inquire
"Who's shaking the ground?" they seem like a fire
I'd somehow ignited, jagged soft sounds
I'd stirred in the water, my hand through fronds
the murmuring grass, a breeze off the pond.

38

The last two swallows swoop down over all
going toward the barn flying from sight.
In ripples of wind out of the west, light
dies in many clouds and in darkness falls
on the pond. Shadows in leaves, the trees grew
black in flat silhouettes against the sky
losing detail, keeping form. Good-bye. I
become invisible myself. A few
fireflies blink, the crickets and katydids
chirr and a frog croaks making me feel it
is my soul. But that's the night. Bats fade, flit.
What I'm writing is vanishing. What was
I thinking? I can't see my way home nor
the branch across my face suddenly formed.

39

This is a place of solace. What's sacred
is partly made by humans. Here's remained
a quiet glade forgotten and unclaimed
till my brother found it while he hunted.
Who would want to leave it? In the woods, old
as a hundred years or more, sandstone carved
and laid with great care is circling the dark
spring's bubbles that are churning the sand cold.
Constantly moving—it will never freeze—
the water is delicious, wide and deep
where I've come down the steps to kneel and steep
my hand cupped and about to drink at ease
and at peace with my brother standing there
a quiet man even quieter here.

41

At any moment it's going to rain
making the world for miles around all wet.
As the sky's growing darker the leaves get
anxious—Or is it me? No I remain
calm on this comfortable rock and see
it's the branches above start to rustle.
Crickets chirring whir. Wild anise tussles
with the wind while the butterflies and bees
cling to its blue petals. Delicious leaves!
I chew on one; it's sweet as the first drops
hit my shoulder quick as bullets—Cold stops
me from writing this. Yow! Where was I? Geeze
it's like I bleed. My pencil tears the page.
Here I have to stop and let the storm rage.

44

I hear Dad's chainsaw echo down the field
cutting firewood for December's stove. Her
knife in hand, Mom chops the cabbage she'll seal
in jars, pouring boiling water over
it first with a tablespoon of sea salt.
Come November she'll have her sauerkraut.
Summer yet, but going, and not the fault
of summer that it goes. I want to shout
"Don't go!" but that won't stop its going though and
feel it in my bones. I put away the
stuff that stays and pack the stuff that goes. A
wasp falls down along the windowpane and
curls up on the windowsill. Leaves burn
and swallows go before they can return.

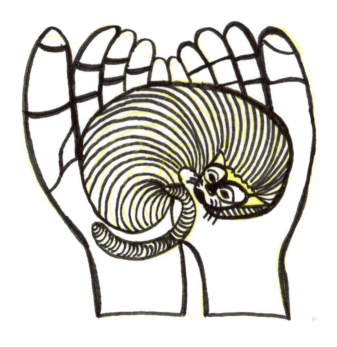

47

Come on, Old Sun, I'm rooting for you. Please
break from the clouds and make the morning warm.
Send all the rainy cold up north to freeze
the melting icebergs and undo the storm
about to come. Let me get something done
if one small task. Let it be good. Inform
the Fates to grace today. Let work be fun.
I'm only human, vulnerable flesh
and blood. There's lots to do. Let me choose one
job to concentrate on and accomplish.
Around me is a forest full of trees
where I have come to clear a little brush.
Help me see the briar from the berry,
what to let live and destroy completely.

50

I am singular and we are plural.
I see us walking on the busy street
and waiting for the bus. Each day I meet
him, Walt Whitman, whose kind face I see all
over the place. Or I am in his brain
because I think that poet isn't dead
anymore than I live. Grass in his stead
comes through the sidewalk's cracks. Let it remain
unnoticed as the air we breathe. New York
City is just a poet's thought and we
are written on the page eternally
living then as well as now. Yet time's short.
It's important to talk and say what is.
I think of him. I am a thought of his.

51

The sun is going down. In New York Town
the tugboat tugs the barge with all its might
the young boy does a wheelie on his bike
the currents of the river swell with sound
it's really getting dark, but there is light
on the water and the sky reflected
in bright ripples along the west, not red
in this sunset, but a radiant white
that glows among the topless spires and spreads
to give all of southern Manhattan life
going where it goes without any strife.
How easy it does seem to die. That said
mustn't cry. Happiness makes us fearless.
We're light and go with light no more no less.

53

It's in the doing that you get the strength
to continue what you do and succeed
at last. Experience is what you need
and if too young for that, then faith at length
will get you where you want to go, step at
a time, when heart and mind are one. If not
the heart will start to go, but then will stop
never wanting what the mind wants. My cat
contented sleeps away the morning while
I write carefully carelessly.
I'm not perfect. I make mistakes I see
and cross out. I don't erase. I smile. My
pencil's lead ends before the eraser.
Cross it out and go on. It's easier.

55

I'm cleaning into every corner.
I don't want any dust. When I am through
the sun will shine in clear windows and you
will see the majestic willows over
across the street are looking back at us.
I promise. You used to see the World
Trade Center from this room. It kind of whirled
around and then was gone, a lot of dust
covering us, smoke and a burnt bad smell
but that was long ago though a busy
city like Manhattan is always dirty
so when somebody sweeps it, you can tell.
Like editing words, clearing clutter shows
honest as a poem the surface below.

60

None of my CDs are in their proper
covers and I can't find the song I want.
Outside a dog is barking, barking. Why
won't it stop? The day is dark and dreary
raining wet and cold. I will need a huge
umbrella wherever I go. Details
dictate what I do and I know I must
watch out. I'm peeling an onion now.
This layer's rotten, what follows is not.
Here some may stop and not peel back the truth
of what turns out to be good for future
nourishment. Why fault a little onion
and curse and rue the day? Hear sad Billie
Holiday sing happily come what may.

61

Things are often more beautiful at a
distance, but not you. The closer the more
inevitable you become. Before
I thought beauty was what I saw, that the
superficial awed, but I was wrong. Your
skin is really you as fragrant as the
rose whose tenderness exudes its soul. A
truth is always true. I am no longer
young and though I know you would like to kiss
you must think of the future and begin.
Love though sinless would be completely sin
if from your lovely limbs more loveliness
doesn't spring. This spring is my sacrifice
and joins me with you in begetting life.

62

Bird in the tree you are singing to me
as if you know and care that I am here
each note intended to put in my ear
a song. What is alone can be pretty
sharing itself, staccato before the
profound pause and silence still near and far.
Unseen the melody is all you are
bird off on some limb that is budding a
leaf as I write listening and the winds
and other choruses, even the car
screeching its brakes do not startle, just are.
The cat licks the hair on my leg and winds
around a thigh, it too meaning one thing
this sonnet is taking shape while you sing.

66

My Spanish-speaking students ask me where
the English language comes from and I tell
them the Anglo-Saxons. But the conquest
of England by France made their native tongue
lower class, so crude and illiterate
that even to this day *fuck, fart* and *shit*
aren't said in polite society. We're
ashamed and self-hating hearing our Dame
English is partly French. I ask, "Is there
any French in Spanish like *rapprochement*
or *double entendre*?" Adamantly
they shake their heads no, no, till one student
looks at the rest and says, "There's *déjà vu*."
They have to agree: "*Déjà vu*, that's true."

67

I used to clean cat vomit up but now
I don't unless it's in the path I walk.
Otherwise it can stay, unlike broken
glass or garbage with day-old fish in it.
In less than an hour or less than that
the cat comes back to lick and eat it up.
You have to have the patience to leave it
forgotten as you should an argument
on politics. To change your mind you must
change yourself and some people are afraid
to be someone else. Have you ever met
a racist who's not stupid? I haven't.
Sad but true, you can't make a rock into
a jewel no matter how you want to.

68

Had I left sooner or later it would
all have been different, but I didn't
and got into two arguments, one in
a store and one on the sidewalk about
the neighborhood with two freeloaders who
do nothing, yet want something for nothing.
Today is Good Friday. You know something?
The world's violent. I stop at a stoop
to scribble this on the only piece of
paper that I have, using the back of
a pack of batteries on the flat of
the cardboard, what space I can make use of.
A young man leaving looks at me askance
as if I'm someone crazy here by chance.

73

Loose pencils make everything dirty
rubbing against them. If you don't contain
them in a box in your bag don't complain
because you have to expect that really
and can't begrudge the smudge. Gladly I sit
with this uncontained pencil of mine, write
that this high rocky mile that I've just climbed
measures more than the mile as I walk it
in the city from school house to flat park.
I love New York, don't get me wrong, but way
up the mountain on a rock I can take
off my clothes for a little while and start
to rest until the rain and cold make me
dress again. There's nothing like nudity.

74

I saw the bluebird first, its beating soft
red breast. Young water snake, I looked for it
next settled near the dock, but it hadn't
risen yet or already'd slithered off.
The pond's cold. I won't dive in. It is flogged
by nasty winds abstractly shattering
the sky on its surface like leaves fluttering
while real fallen ones nearby jump like frogs.
I'm so happy I can't believe my eyes.
The barn swallows have returned from the south
coming like a promised kiss on the mouth.
Friends are welcome even when a surprise.
Pleasant remembered all but forgotten
thoughts bring the warm sun with them when they come.

79

A squirrel just walked across my shoulder
like I wasn't there and didn't matter
part of the bench, a kind of nothingness
who thought for a moment that a hand pressed
on him like an old friend's familiar
enough to touch, but that was peculiar
and much more likely a panhandler's strange
and intruding about to ask for change
or could it be that suddenly a crazy
man was going to start to strangle me?
Calmly getting ready for a fight I
saw the bushy tail right between my eyes
not a friend's or beggar's fingers uncurled
no murderer's. Death shrank into a squirrel.

82

I'm cooking while I write this sonnet
poaching asparagus sprinkling them all
with some chili powder shaking the stalks
squeezing on a lemon. These tastes will set
and mix as the vegetables lose steam
and begin to chill. Heat, boil chicken broth
an onion and garlic. Spoon off the froth.
Dice tomatoes and dump that in. Then clean
chop parsley and watercress together.
Wait letting the soup reduce simmering.
Kill the fire as you drop the herbs in
to enhance their color and their flavor.
Overcooked food fades on the tongue. Food's heard.
Say *bread*. You see and smell and taste the word.

84

My only brother with his bulldozer
pushed the brush away from the day lilies
uprooting thorns and sumac completely
around the bed revealing for mother
those common flowers in all their glory.
Now if only she'll come to look at them
making her way to the lower yard and
sitting on the old swing near the swamp see
how the hard green stalk shooting up becomes
a flame in flames just like the fireworks
are going to explode on July 4th.
Look, here she comes to watch the explosions
as the night with a swallow swoops above.
Nothing animates us more than love.

86

As I put my nose in milkweed blossoms
their resemblance to lilacs reminding
me now of the cold early spring sniffing
up the heavy fragrance happily some
bees move around me in such a good mood
none of them try to sting and keep humming
along my skin and the flower grazing
and finding there what will be honey food.
Fluttering butterfly startling my eyes
sticks its slender black thin proboscis in
the abundant overflowing. Walking
home patchouli's in the air, a surprise
that's wonderful because I like the smell
but if you don't, it must be living hell.

87

She completely sparkles, the girl talking
to her father in a conversation
that must be a little funny because
she starts to laugh as well as talk, talking
of her final destination perhaps
leaving this very morning on a trip
from Lancaster on the platform going
east to Philadelphia, New York and
every other point. Then her mother
who's been watching men working on the tracks
finally joins in and starts to point this
way and that—Which way is the train coming?
Each wears a shirt a shade of blue, the girl's
with stars. Above the sky is blue. Clouds swirl.

88

At the wedding not only the living
but the dead are also here and all those
who aren't born yet here I suppose because
there are more of them than us, the living
with the sea and pines to our right and left
ghost relatives and babies yet to bloom.
Life is a garden seeded by the groom.
At Pat and Grace's wedding I was Best
Man. There I gave a toast about the love
that had brought all of us close together
a love that's still bringing us together.
I see old friends Tony and Sylvia
sit, the past present. Here comes the bride. Wow!
We stand and all look back to what is now.

89

We'd be just as comfortable naked
but put on swimming suits anyway just
in case some hikers should come and find us
sunning by the stream. The unexpected
often happens watching what's all around.
You point out the bright cardinal flower
and I the heron that looms before our
eyes gone in the lumbering air unbound.
We talk of favorite authors, Catullus
Whitman, Hawthorne, intimate as lovers.
I wish that I'd brought some Willa Cather.
If only you'd come to read her, I trust
you'll find her as I do, that violet
there clinging to the cliff. Do you see it?

90

The poet slides on her bottom stubborn
as a turtle over slippery stones
sitting inching picking up the large ones
that hinder her path dropping them to form
an island in the current that's rushing
at us. I'm on the stream's descending slope
walking as best I can, wavering, grope
ready to fall and hurt myself getting
safely up to my waist and then my neck.
"What do you call that flower?" "Jewel Weed."
"It's beautiful. I think we're in Eden."
"We are. I can see a snake," Bernadette
says—it is peeking from the rocks—and glides
spreading out her arms swimming by my side.

91

Cooking something is like you're saying it
saying just what you think when you make food
I mean give words to it. Poets are good
cooks. Even after her stroke Bernadette
can still bake a chicken, prepare and stick
it in the oven, bring it out just right.
Phil grills sausage and sets them in our sights
thick sensual ready to bite. Who mixed
the salad with herbs from the woods and greens
chilled and tossed naked with fresh vinaigrette?
Who put the bread and cheese here? Bernadette!
I cut lemons, my fingers straining seeds
squeeze over ice and vodka, no small feat.
Reader, join us if you want to. Let's eat!

92

To be understood words are objective
yet we understand them subjectively.
When Willa Cather writes, "The long main street
began at the church, the town seemed to flow
from it like a stream from a spring," the prose
forms naturally from the simile.
Do you feel it as I do when I read
that words not only are but also live?
From church to street to town to spring as if
the stream itself were writing the sentence.
Cather is here with me in the present
bringing from the past continuous gifts
words that are as real as the broken fence
I built with Dad to keep the horses in.

93

On a road of crushed salamanders, snakes
and butterflies I make my weary way
listening to a woman sing who makes
Mali her home thousands of miles away.
In Pennsylvania Africa's close
as the green limbs that are brushing my limbs
when I pick their acorns from them. The toad
skins under car wheels pressed in macadam
resemble Roman mosaics. I pass
mosaics of grasshoppers. Catullus
breathed molecules of air I breathe and pass.
I want to hear the yellow jackets buzz
on a corpse and turning the music down
hear the airplane above, a louder sound.

94

Last year my father had a little stroke.
"Merry Christmas," he says and then corrects
himself: "Happy Christmas." That's a mistake
he realizes after he says it
and lowers his head. This in reference
to my own birth on August the 15th
which is today. How many important
and unimportant facts come crowd our heads
to their eminentest extents added
the very first minute we remembered
the word to say exactly what we meant?
Oh where is it? The word I need to name
both you and me. "Happy Birthday," Daddy
finally says laughing triumphantly.

105

I let down the umbrella on the dock
enclosing the wasps inside who've summered
up in the ribs. I had to do it. Not
only is it sunset but September
the summer is almost over and I
must go back to New York to work to live.
I'm sorry, guys. Unsettled now they fly
around my head, yet still stay off. We lived
let live. They came and went while I below
wrote and read without incident. Black wasps
are curious, not inclined to sting though
walking on your skin. Even now not cross
accepting it as soon they will the cold
back and forth they go settling in new folds.

106

Today I picked Uncle Al's tomatoes
for the last time. Many were overripe
rotten, had cracked or fallen. I was tired
but constant and making an effort to
exercise, bent holding my abdomen
in reaching into the vines to find them
ready and easily pulled from their stems
taking a lot of green ones putting them
at the bottom of the baskets. When in
New York I will give some to friends and keep
the rest for as long as I possibly
can because there is no better eating
than a tomato from a man who knows
how to plant it well and make it grow.

107

I created the world with the first word
I spoke connecting myself with the real.
Then I could even close my eyes and feel
what I'd set in motion with the first word
I had spoken. Perhaps it was water
perhaps it was a snake or sun coming
through the branches. Right now I'm creating
because I was told to by Bill Kushner.
His hands look like sandstone with sudden flecks
of pink in them, asterisk fingertips
or constellations of stars. From his lips
he commands, "Write," and my hand starts to, quick
blurred. It's difficult to see what's living.
Is it from the dead we get our bearings?

109

Out of the ordinary there will come
from time to time the good and very brave
extraordinary, someone who can save
us from our own damned selves and make us one
humanity. Children take Rosa Parks
for an example, a common seamstress
who sat herself down in a seat she was
told she couldn't. Some said she was too dark.
Justice became evident and the fact
that a quiet woman can unsever
people divided, sew them together
nobody free till all are freed at last.
One little candle gives light to the night.
Truth is simple. It's visible. It's sight.

III

Almost December, Thanksgiving over
outside is frozen once again. The warm
TV is on and logs burn in the stove.
I am eating Aunt Fern's dried tomatoes
desiccated skins like mummies from the
pyramids. Yum Yum Yum all of her love's
ripe on my tongue as I soften them up
moistening spots, the harvest of August.
Suddenly last summer is in my mouth.
Katydids and fireflies live in the spit
and what had seemed hard and dead's a red sweet
salamander slipping between my teeth—
Just one of the things Aunt Fern's gift is
I'd be satisfied if this were heaven.

113

On a milkweed pod there is a tuft of
seeded fluff clinging like a terrified
hysteric dangling from a cliff. I huff
and puff but it won't let go and take flight
from its husk, dry and brittle broken stuff
that it clutches desperately to stay
holding on till my breath blows strong enough
to send it off. Up, out it goes—Away!
Then like an inconsistent memory
or second thought it spins and turns around
coming back down from where it came now free
to idle in the leaves on the cold ground
where any birth seems to be frozen yet
white and trembling and resembling death.

114

Dusk comes as I look at the Egyptian
temple by the reflection pool and the
crocodile, pink-flecked marble circa 1
A.D. as old as Christ and older than
me. It was a cold walk from the subway
cold as this smooth stone I am sitting on
near a father holding his happy son's
hand dangling from him at an angle. Hey
when this boy's as old as I am I'll be
dead and that old temple there will still stand
just as it is in mid-town Manhattan
unless some comet hits us or the sea
has risen. Mundane facts keep us present
forgetting, remembering the moment.

115

Light comes down on Saint Francis through the cleft.
The Illuminator we do not see
only the Illuminated who bleeds
out of his hands. My friend Bill Kushner left
the hospital this morning at long last
the noon sun shining down on his bright pate.
The poet asks himself, "Is it too late
to start again? Should I forget it? Fast
life goes on whether I do or I don't
make it to the cab at the corner. Fuck it.
I might as well write another sonnet.
Just what the world needs, another poem."
The poet lives unwanted and then is
wanted when dead. Home is where the light is.

116

"How old is your son?" "He is 9 o'clock,"
my student says and the class laughs as well
it should. My student laughs and cannot stop
nor can anyone. We laugh and the spell
goes on unbroken. Everyone shakes
in on the joke, happy to be sharing
understanding the premise and mistake.
Laughter engenders laughter as kissing
kisses: just watch the teenagers do it
on the park bench. Laughter is forever.
That's why Buddha laughs. It was expensive,
my old sweater. Cachito clings closer
sticking his nails in. Let the cat claw it.
What the heck. Life goes on and Death doesn't.

118

Over the ferns and the treacherous rocks
popping out of the steep ground like the heads
of dinosaurs I come watching my steps
so I won't fall or slip or have to stop
till I'm drinking at the falls where the stream
comes splashing down the mountain. What I see
I remember when I was three looking
in this stream on a winter's day. Daddy
carried me most of the way. I wasn't sick
just cold from the snow. Minnows were swimming.
How could that be, the world frozen but in
the spring the fishes swim? It was magic.
Life was no different than a fairy
tale I understood immediately.

120

Pat, Happy Birthday on your sixtieth.
I really would like this little sonnet
to be one of the greetings that you get
embracing you and giving you a kiss.
So much more does happen in the past than
in the present. Time keeps moving, adding
on more to us. Natural as breathing
a breath are two friends when they meet again
talking of what's gone on and what it's meant
since they last met. No other tongue can tell
what friends say now. Here is wishing you well.
The past is not the past when you're present.
Not only has it been good to know you
but you are something to look forward to.

121

Out of the old dead roots comes life itself.
Milkweed shoots shooting up from the cold ground
have made my mourning happy to have found
them here unfolding leaves out of themselves.
Where do we go after we've departed?
I've been wanting to find her, my old teacher.
She told me I could write, my believer.
Without her there wouldn't be any art.
Now that she's gone I want to walk and talk
again along this mountain road. We'd see
in sprouting milkweed there is poetry
her words as well as mine these written stalks
a poem where she has gone. We'd talk of how
one way or the other life is travel.

123

It is so hot before you run you sweat.
Fanning himself a man and his wife walk
holding hands. He sings and she doesn't with
just as much force. It's dawn. The lighter it
gets the more the runners start to come. The
man shooting baskets soon is many all
caught up shouting and jumping for the ball.
Other arrivals lift their arms and bend
touching their toes before they start to run
calling to each other words I don't know.
All I can say's "Good morning" and "Hello."
I can't read one word that's on the wall, none.
There are more words than anyone can learn.
Most stories go untold as the world turns.

127

"Teacher, I don't know what a pig pen is."
"What's a pen?" "This is a pen," some students
say showing them. "That pen contains ink. Pens
can contain pigs. Pig pen. Ink pen." "Ink is
a noun just like a pen is. How can nouns
be adjectives?" "English is an easy
language that uses one word for many
things. We pen stories and pen the pig." Now
still seeing some puzzled faces I draw
a swirled tail on the board connecting a
rump to a back, ear, and head until a
pig appears. The class laughs seeing me draw
two vertical lines through horizontal
ones fencing that pig in once and for all.

129

The students look amazed or perplexed at
us American teachers who have stopped
to surround a ragged little dog with
matted hair that's starved to the bone. Corliss
pours water on the steps for it to drink.
I have a boiled egg in my pack and crack
it open trying to separate shell
from egg breaking it up and scattering
it. The dog aware of yolk starts to eat
leaving the white—Can a hungry dog do
this? The custodian comes with a broom.
He's mad as hell. He's pissed. Don't we get it?
It's going to die and we have left a mess.
We might be teachers, but we're idiots.

131

The quiet aftermath of disaster
dangling in the sunlight in a tall tree
only decay to ever come after
falling apart vanishing in the breeze
where every now and then someone looks up
to wonder what it was that went so wrong
that what should be below is there above
not high up in the sky but upside-down.
Kite with a tail of yellow, blue and pink
triangles entangled in the branches
is sagging on its string—Who'd ever think
such a beautiful thing could end like this?
I know that whatever the reason is
it doesn't belong there, but there it is.

138

As swallows swoop above the boat begins
to move although all of us people here
stay still hearing the horn announce we have
let go. The leaves of the rooted bamboo
bend and sway. Mountains go back and further
back into the clouds. The little boy's foot's
tapping as he plays his computer game.
He is entranced as I am watching him.
Oh to be a kid again! There are things
I'll never know, but I can see the wind
that turns the page turns the wave as the night
begins to turn the day darkening me
and the fluttering lady next to me
turning to throw her rind in the Yangtze.

139

Out of the dark the steep mountains come. At
first a line and nothing more appears on
either side for a long time then there's light
inside a house, someone asleep who woke.
I am all alone along the Yangtze
whose sides are high, pure rock. No one lives there
but singing birds awake before the sun
gives shape to where they sing. I see passing
towns put here before the waters rise to
house millions of displaced inhabitants
time will eventually cover after
all like water or the clouds covering
the mountaintops that also seem to press
us down into the present world's contents.

141

The woman in pink by the lotus pool
seems like a flower herself. Her wide straw hat
hides her face, keeps her anonymous. That
could be a man. No sun today. It's cool.
The crop is abundant and overflows
its banks disguising the water and land
where the land is as flat as a pool and
one place is as green as another. Go
but always be careful and when you step
remember. Notice where the woman is
where the ox will only stretch out its neck
and that one heron is always present.
Then you won't fall in where the bountiful
lotus rises to feed both wise and fool.

142

The obligatory bit of struggling
out of the arms of comrades into the
arms of chaos, customs, checking luggage
departing which is also arriving.
Suddenly strangers seem significant
until you remember where you're going
as you're forgetting where you've been putting
on the seat belt wondering if we're meant
today to live. Who's that sitting over
there? A terrorist? Clouds are in the sky
ocean's in the ocean and there is my
Manhattan below me. There's the Chrysler
Building and La Plaza Cultural. There's
where my home's been for almost thirty years.

143

Goldfinch balanced on the sunflower's head
flies off swaying the plant just like the wind.
The sun comes up the trees and lies down in
the field where a red hawk begins to spread
its great slow wings breaking from the branch. Cloud
like Magritte's so real I feel it's a round
cotton above my head to swab a wound
if one occurs. Near the barn I've allowed
Cachito to examine groundhog holes.
Hey, Cachito, groundhogs are really fat
but they can fight. Watch out! Ah, but a cat's
a cat and lives like that. I think we all
do things that get a lot better and change
yet like the cat stay pretty much the same.

144

The crows go calling, "There is bread, there is
bread in the field, hot dog buns that have been
thrown by a man who doesn't seem to want
them." It's startling how the news travels
fast. Suddenly black wings break up the air.
What seemed so far is really near. More than
what's good becomes a happy memory.
We are born and are who we are because
we were loved or loved and beaten or just
beaten like so many colored pebbles
that are shaken and come to rest in a
jar. I'm glad I've thrown the bread causing all
of this commotion coming from the pines
and sky. The cawing's comforting; it's mine.

145

As I'm editing my China Journal
across from me on the horizontal
flat amputated willow branch perches
a red-tailed hawk that's just caught a flopping
pigeon whose soft breast feathers it starts to
pluck out to get at the heart. Some people
wondering what others are looking at
look up themselves and for a moment stop
what they are doing, the baby strollers
parked in neutral, dogs on leashes waiting
for their masters. Children on the way to
school dance in the fine feathers falling down.
One child jumps up to catch the floating stuff
and gives it to another with a hug.

147

I am alive and you are dead. Here on
my end the conversation hasn't
quite ended but judging by the silence
on yours it has. A cloudy day is
here for now, dark afternoon, April snow
flitting by the window, hurrying ghosts
going home. When the frogs at dusk begin
to sing for love in the smoking pools, it
would be absolutely great to talk of
anything—a poet, the Romantics,
Keats, Coleridge, Wordsworth—But it's too late.
No more! Today's a stone. And it is cold!
George W. Bush is still president.
Oh even to sit and complain of him!

148

These sonnets have been difficult to write
enough to begin and not finish. They've
lain like skeletons—a little finger
a little skull—stuck in a drawer. Are they
rotting or taking form, flesh come to bone
or corpse? I have almost given up hope
treat my liver for Hepatitis C
with an injection once a week, six pills
a day that tire and overwhelm me with
worthlessness. Everything turns to shit
stinks and vanishes. The poet's verses
addressing the flower and tomb born well
or beheaded one day won't be thought of
even as you read this with the knowledge.

150

I wake the snakes on the way to the lake
coiling in leaves, slithering at my feet
half-seen in the low branches, thick brown waists
headless, tailless stone still in wait for me
to trip them into slithering again.
Are they going to bite? I doubt it
they're enjoying themselves too much and slide
on in the fear and excitement of my
approaching steps. Without ever really
seeing them slip into the rippling depths
on the briar's edge of the round abyss
water snakes have taken the day with them.
Here comes the night. Everything fades from sight.
A frog peeps. There is sound, song but no light.

151

My feet are resting in the alfalfa.
Bumblebees cover and bend the blossoms
even further down than the warm wind is
blowing through them. Out on the water
reflected transitory clouds turn light
into shadows over me and the world
around. Perfectly still dragonfly's whirled
to the back of my hand. Big round black eyes
loom up and shine bigger than its body
a thin blue crooked breathing stick attached
to transparent wings full of dark veins that
move together and apart then quickly
go leaving me here alone with the woods
on one side and on the other the pond.

157

There is almost nothing left of it, a
solitary tortuous—no, tortured—
stem, twisted pods at the tip of the rod
broken off, the pinnacle gone, toppled
but not completely down; it's still holding
on by a thread wound round itself sticking
to the stalk, dried up tufts that never got
to float in the wind but stayed stuck instead
though most of their dark seeds have fallen now
germinating in the very same ground
where they were born. I write this with a script
so cold and thin and sloppily written
if I don't rewrite it when I get home
no one will ever know what I just wrote.

158

Like the dried up dead wasp with its venom
gone rolled up on the windowsill like a
ball of dust my mother slumbers with her
head bent near a bowl of fruit Pat Maples
sent listening to Ella Fitzgerald
sing, a dying lady and a dead one
sharing the moment I am sharing too
taking a break from the navy bean soup
hambone left over from Christmas dinner
with its stock simmering in celery
carrots and onions. *The trembling trees
embrace the breeze tenderly* is really
not true on this stark dark December day
—No, the music's always true while it plays.

159

The beauty of the words comes partly by
intent, partly instinct, by what's given
a gift. So's the luck we artists get. Go
where you want to go and really go there
in the direction you are going. Do
your painting or sculpting or singing a
song, whatever it is you are leaving
behind, your worthy thoughts. Daddy's leaving
land and a pond. Mother is leaving me.
Ladybugs leave more ladybugs crawling
everywhere, well, not everywhere
but if you look there's one on the ceiling
one by the light. The fire leaves ash, goes out.
Cachito meows. I leave you reading now.

161

My nephew has long fingers that can spread
to B major where the B major is.
You only learn guitar by playing it
and Daniel is more dedicated
than I am but I keep playing the chords
I know and they all do turn out somehow
Bury Me Under the Weeping Willow
which we're going to perform for mother
pretty soon. The rain's pitter-patter
on the roof and the apple tree shaking
its branches against the window wanting
to come in and join us are our comrades
in this endeavor. Each sound has a say
becoming a part of the song we play.

172

The one-headed doe drinking becomes two
heads reflected in the pond. Now the third
one jumps and dashes, splashes with its hooves
this youngest one especially happy
enjoying itself. More than anything
I love when unexpected creatures come
unaware till they though not I have had
enough and turn to leave, their heads going
into the trees, backs and rumps the bushes
shivering goldenrod. Right now the sky
is recollecting itself immense and
unfathomable as it's always been
since I can remember peaceful and blue
allowing one butterfly to pass through.

176

There was a transitory spider's web
clinging to a metaphoric branch of
birch that I undid stupidly touching
it as I was going down the mountain
side, the troubled spider in the middle
clinging to a strand of its work in the
wind. Happily I see what I had hoped
to see climbing back up. The web is here
again. Dear spider, you do not know how
glad I am that you've done what I'd undone
delicate, strong and glistening. These words
will be a signpost telling the passer
not to reach for your tantalizing string.
The poem touches and leaves it hanging.

179

In the devastating cold early spring
I watch the vultures glide from one side of
the sky to the other. There's a stalk of
dried up milkweed over a log leaning
uprooted with half a pod still on, its
seeds like every word in a poem
that were yearning to take form have fallen
on fertile ground. So little's green now. Just
babies yet, the leaves of a common weed
begin to peek—How they will grow and reach
and spread to the size of elephant ears
which is what we used to call them when we
were kids pulling them out with great flappings
imagining what it's like to have wings.

180

I hear the geese at first far off flying
in the distance and curious look up
to find them near the horizon slanting
forward like sentences being written
across the sky in honking changing lines
until they're gone. Over the rocks the stream
at Walnut Run splashes down clogged with sticks
from last year's storms. Minnows nose up this flow
like ripples they swim in below fooling
predators. Everything begins to grow.
At the corner of my eye dead leaves
shake on a branch that seems dead too except
at the very end of every stem
sharp golden buds are ready to open.

ACKNOWLEDGMENTS

Sonnet 28 was published in *Literati Quarterly*. Sonnets 66, 67, 115, 127, and 176 were published in *The Brooklyn Rail*. Sonnets 62 and 86 were published in *Zocalo Public Square*.

AUTHOR STATEMENT

After writing no poems for twenty years, the idea of writing sonnets occurred to me shortly after the invasion of Iraq in 2003—I think because I opposed the invasion so much I needed something I could control, and what better way than working with a form I had never worked with before. *Spring Sonnets* are ninety sonnets chosen from the first one hundred and eighty written from the spring of 2003 until the spring of 2009. My goal is to write three hundred and sixty, like the degrees in a circle. I have two hundred and forty written so far, which happily leaves me more to do and the reader hopefully more to look forward to.

INDEX OF FIRST LINES

A cawing crow gets louder and louder, 24
A squirrel just walked across my shoulder, 46
Almost December, Thanksgiving over, 62
As I put my nose in milkweed blossoms, 49
As I'm editing my China Journal, 82
As swallows swoop above the boat begins, 76
At any moment it's going to rain, 29
At the wedding not only the living, 51
Bird in the tree you are singing to me, 40
Come on, Old Sun, I'm rooting for you. Please, 33
Cooking something is like you're saying it, 54
Dusk comes as I look at the Egyptian, 66
Every time I come it is the same, stream, 2
Goldfinch balanced on the sunflower's head, 80
Had I left sooner or later it would, 43
How old is your son? He is 9 o'clock, 68
I am alive and you are dead. Here on, 83
I am singular and we are plural, 34
I created the world with the first word, 60
I hear Dad's chainsaw echo down the field, 30
I hear the geese at first far off flying, 94
I let down the umbrella on the dock, 58
I overturned the rowboat planning soon, 26
I saw the bluebird first, its beating soft, 45
I see how strong a fragile thing can be, 25
I used to clean cat vomit up but now, 42
I wake the snakes on the way to the lake, 85
I'm cleaning into every corner, 37
I'm cooking while I write this sonnet, 47
I'm happy when the day begins and I'm, 12
In the devastating cold early spring, 93
In the early dewdrop chilly morning, 22

It is snowing, it snowed, and it will snow, 13
It is so hot before you run you sweat, 72
It's in the doing that you get the strength, 36
Jimmy, you let your dogs shit where they want, 4
Last year my father had a little stroke, 57
Light comes down on Saint Francis through the cleft, 67
Like the dried up dead wasp with its venom, 88
Looking at the springs, sitting in the sun, 1
Loose pencils make everything dirty, 44
My cat and I play chasing each other, 20
My feet are resting in the alfalfa, 86
My hands are numb and yet the sun is bright, 15
My nephew has long fingers that can spread, 90
My only brother with his bulldozer, 48
My Spanish-speaking students ask me where, 41
None of my CDs are in their proper, 38
On a milkweed pod there is a tuft of, 65
On a road of crushed salamanders, snakes, 56
Out of the dark the steep mountains come. At, 77
Out of the old dead roots comes life itself, 71
Out of the ordinary there will come, 61
Over the ferns and the treacherous rocks, 69
Pat, Happy Birthday on your sixtieth, 70
She completely sparkles, the girl talking, 50
Silent morning, about to rain. Birds sing, 3
Teacher, I don't know what a pig pen is, 73
The beauty of the words comes partly by, 89
The butterflies of spring are small and dark, 17
The crows go calling, There is bread, there is, 81
The flies and itching heat are gone at last, 6
The fortunate fish escaped from the net, 18
The last two swallows swoop down over all, 27
The obligatory bit of struggling, 79
The one-headed doe drinking becomes two, 91

The poet slides on her bottom stubborn, 53
The quiet aftermath of disaster, 75
The setting sun and I are way above, 14
The students look amazed or perplexed at, 74
The sun is going down. In New York Town, 35
The woman in pink by the lotus pool, 78
There is almost nothing left of it, a, 87
There was a transitory spider's web, 92
These sonnets have been difficult to write, 84
Things are often more beautiful at a, 39
This is a place of solace. What's sacred, 28
To be understood words are objective, 55
Today for the first time in my whole life, 23
Today I picked Uncle Al's tomatoes, 59
We met by chance in a shadowy place, 8
We'd be just as comfortable naked, 52
When I put headphones on it's like I'm deaf, 9
When I think of all the lovers I've had, 5
Work will overcome evil like the grass, 11
Writing's a thing of opposites, putting, 21
You weren't the sort of friend to come and go, 7

ABOUT THE AUTHOR

Don Yorty is a poet, educator, and garden activist living in New York City. He is the author of two previous poetry collections, *A Few Swimmers Appear* and *Poet Laundromat* (both from Philadelphia Eye & Ear), and he is included in *Out of This World, An Anthology of the Poetry of the St. Mark's Poetry Project, 1966–1991*. His novel *What Night Forgets* was published by Herodias Press in 2000. He blogs at donyorty.com: an archive of current art, his own writing, and work of other poets.

ABOUT INDOLENT BOOKS

Founded in 2015, Indolent Books is a nonprofit poetry press based in Brooklyn, with staff working remotely around the country. In our books and on our website, Indolent publishes work by poets and writers who are queer, trans, nonbinary (or gender nonconforming), intersex, women, people of color, people living with HIV, people with histories of addiction, abuse, and other traumatic experiences, and other poets and writers who are underrepresented or marginalized, or whose work has particular relevance to issues of racial, social, economic, and environmental justice. We also focus on poets over 50 without a first book. Indolent is committed to an inclusive workplace. Indolent Books is an imprint of Indolent Arts, a 501(c)(3) charity.

CPSIA information can be obtained
at www.ICGtesting.com
Printed in the USA
LVHW081711170719
624401LV00005B/75/P